THE MOE CHRONICLES

THE MOE CHRONICLES

Tales of a Young Urban Failure

BY ERIK MOE

CHRONICLE BOOKS
SAN FRANCISCO

Library of Congress Cataloging-in-Publication Data:
Moe, Erik.
The Moe chronicles: tales of a young urban failure / by Erik Moe.
p. cm.
ISBN 0-8118-1336-3
I. Title.
PN6727.M63M63 1997
741.5973—dc20 96-6274
CIP

Printed in the United States.

Digital imaging and production by Shauna Middendorf

Distributed in Canada by Raincoast Books
8680 Cambie Street
Vancouver, B.C. V6P 6M9

10 9 8 7 6 5 4 3 2 1

Chronicle Books
275 Fifth Street
San Francisco, CA 94103

To Nanny

Special thanks to: Dave Dakich, Ivo Knezevic, Dave Devencenzi, Brian Bacino, Mary Kilpatrick, Martin Lauber, Peter Rudy, Blake Daley, Jeff Goodby, Rich Silverstein, Steve Sperry, the Moe family, Stu Keith, Doug Allen, Bill Oakley, John Axelburg, John Stephens, Julie Wick, Chip Krauss, Elizabeth Larson, the Rotten Bastards, Paul Renner, and Cathy Anderson.

The other day I went to work.
They'd changed the security code.
Stryker & Duke
Advertising
This is a bad sign.
beep!
beep!

My partner Dave
didn't know it either.
Stryker & Duke
Advertising
This is a really bad sign.
beep!
beep!

We'd been laid off. When we met with the personnel lady she explained there was a restructuring going on.
You have thirty minutes to clean out your offices.

Then we went to the driving range and hit a bucket of balls.
Damn! Another slice.
Thwack!

Being unemployed sucks. The worst part is at night when the voices come.
You're a failure.
You're thirty.
You just ate Ramen Noodles for dinner.

Every day at 10:30 Dave would come over and we'd job hunt.
Alright! Mayberry RFD!
Yessssss!

When you're unemployed you're anxious. You drink a lot of coffee. Mostly you're just really, really bored.
That lady has walked that dog six times today.

You plan to use the extra time to get in shape. You buy sports accessories —and then don't use them.
SPORTS
Jai alai is the sport of the 90's. It's a great aerobic work-out.
I'll take the whole set!
Jai alai Set

You take phone calls from solicitors. And you're interested in what they have to say.
Phil, tell me more about how you can offer such an exciting credit package.

You become inexplicably bitter with employed friends.
So, how do you like my new car?
Oh, it's just great Job-Boy!

Every day at 5:30 we'd go to Kelly's and abuse the Happy Hour privileges.
KELLY'S
You guys want a beer to wash down those four trips to the buffet?
Just water, thanks.

As the weeks stretched into months, depression set in.
Hey! Happy Birthday!
Another day closer to death.

Some days I'd lie around with the curtains drawn listening to Metallica.
Man, these lyrics are soooo true.
Death and Sorrow, Yeah, yeah, yeah

Other days I wouldn't even get out of bed.
What's the point?

But finally, Dave managed to get us an interview at this really cool place.
This is great. How'd you do it?
Lied my ass off

He'd also taken some liberties with our resumes.
AWARD
It's amazing you have so much experience with all our important clients.
It is a coincidence, isn't it?

I couldn't believe it.
The guy offered us jobs.
...and I'm hoping you'll work real hard for us.
Count on it, Chief. Couple of real go-getters, that's us!

Pretty soon, everything was back to normal.
I'm bored.
We should ask for some time off.

I needed a vacation. So a bunch of us took a road trip to the Rose Bowl. My friend Brian played the Counting Crows the whole way.
Rooovund Heeeere!
me driving

We weren't making very good time. We kept having to stop for supplies.
Hey! You just passed a perfectly good Carl's Jr!

And Martin kept getting car sick from riding in the loft.
Dude, next rest stop pull over.
10-4
No one understands what the driver goes through.
101
Ten hours to go? Step on it, Grandma!!

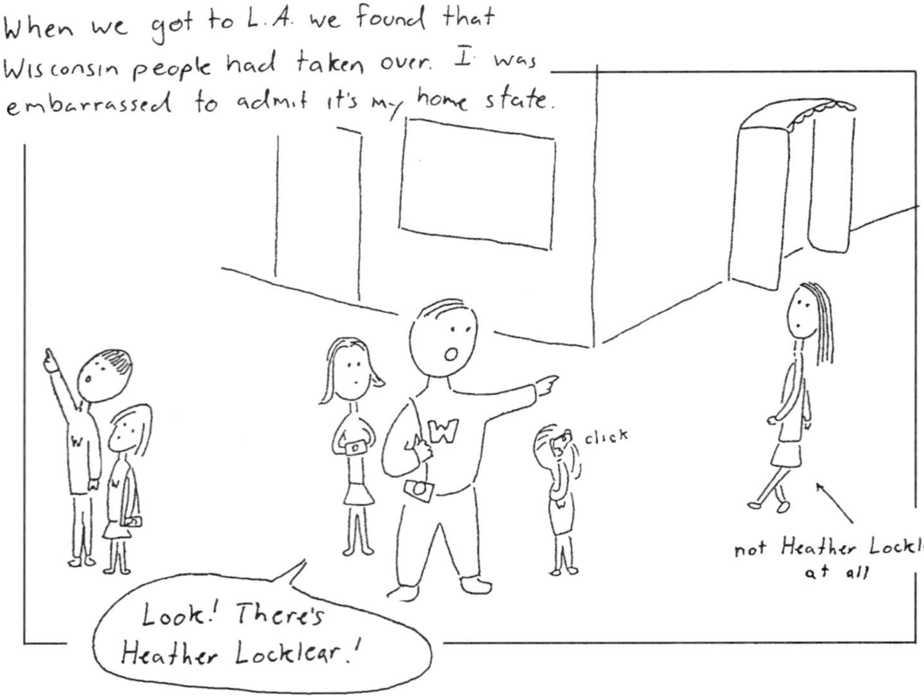

When we got to L.A. we found that Wisconsin people had taken over. I was embarrassed to admit it's my home state.

click

not Heather Locklear at all

Look! There's Heather Locklear!

After the game we went out in Hollywood.
You guys aren't famous. Why are you talking to us?
statuesque model/actress types

We threw a late-night party back at our hotel.
There's no booze left but I found this fluid in the Xerox machine in the lobby.
Hit me.

That year started a lot like the year before.
Take me, God! Take me now!

I made the same resolution, too.
With God as my witness, alcohol shall never touch these lips again!

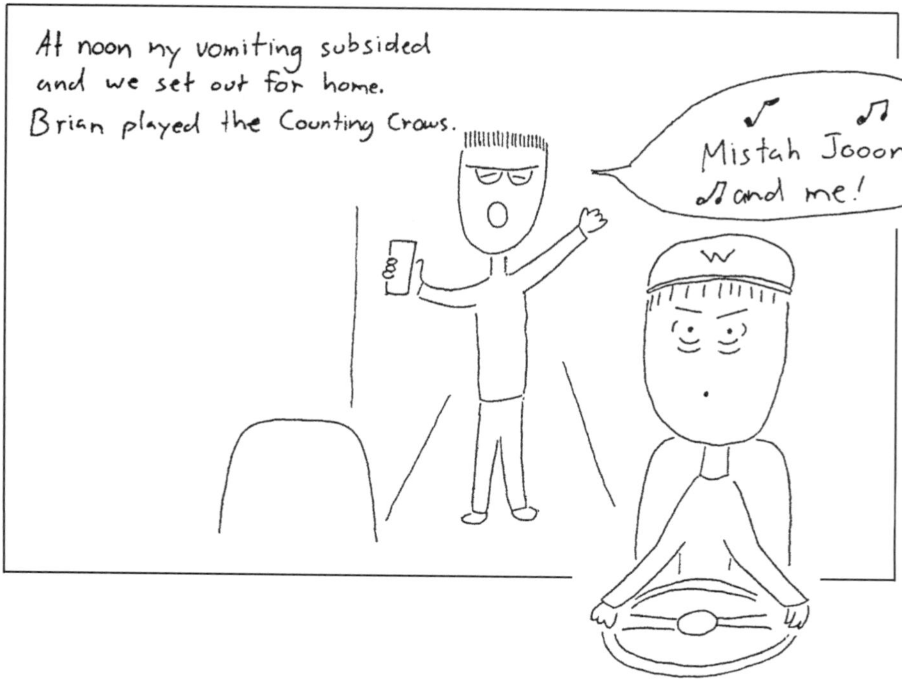

At noon my vomiting subsided and we set out for home. Brian played the Counting Crows.

Mistah Jooones and me!

There's this new girl at work.
She sits by the laser printer.
Just printing out a document. Heh-heh.
Um... great.

I checked around.
She isn't going out with anyone.
And why do you ask?
No reason.

I took her out for lunch. She talked a lot about her roommates.
SUSHI
So then Tina said to Frannie, "You clean the toilet! He's your boy friend..."
You have magnificent hooters.

When I got back, Dave noticed I had a noodle on my face.
Told you to stay away from the Kung Pao Beef.
Rats

There's been a lot of traffic by the laser printer lately.
Don't those guys have any work to do?

The word was getting out. I tried to play a little defense.
Hey! Did you guys see that new babe?!
I heard she has crabs.

One Sunday, I made Dave drive us by her house.
This is really pathetic, man. I can't beli... Hey! There she is!
FLOOR IT!

It was getting to me.
Could you stop that sighing please?

Finally, I got the nerve to ask her out. I thought a group thing would be less stressful.
So anyhoot, Mary, a bunch of us are going to shoot pool tomorrow night and I thought you'd like to come.
squeeze squeeze
You're the guy who sits by the Coke machine, right?

That night I tried my best to impress her. Nothing worked.
Now watch closely, Mare, as I execute my famous triple bank shot with a topspin twist!
Could you introduce me to your friend?
good looking friend Martin

The rest of the night was a blur.
CAB
C'mon, Martin. Let's go!
You don't mind, do you, man?

I got really drunk and slept with her roommate.
Last night was wild! I can't wait to talk about it with Mary.
Oh, God.

After the Mary debacle I decided to reevaluate myself. I took a long look in the mirror.
Spare tire city.
squish
squish

I'm getting fat.
Ladies and gentlemen, a new world record!

So I put on my roller hockey gear and went down to North Beach for a game.
I'll take the guy with the love handles.

I think I'm a little out of shape.
Is that guy okay?
wheeze wheeze
You take him on your team for a while, alright?

I joined a health club.
This is just a preliminary test to determine body fat and... GOOD GOD!!
What? what?!

The guy recommended a weight-training schedule and told me to eat better.
Do Cheetos count as a starch?
79¢
1.19
59¢
CHEETOS

I worked out like a madman for six weeks. I made Dave go too.
You should see your face right now.

Two hours a day, five days a week. I was totally focused.
Butt floss at eleven o'clock
Got it.

For some reason,
when you work out regularly
you feel the need to
discuss it with others.
...and then I'll probably
work on my abs...
Mmmm, hmm.

You feel superior
to the unfit.
Tsk, tsk.
Will you just look
at that poor guy?
munch
munch

I knew I was looking good. So one day I stopped by the ol' laser printer.
Notice anything about me, Mare?
Um.... no.

It felt good to be back in the saddle again.
CHEETOS
Shut up, Alex
No, you shut up, Mallory!

Last week, my old buddy Peter came for a visit. It was a good distraction from Mary... for a while.
Dude, if you want I'll tape "Sally" for you.
Cool.
CHIPS

The weekend stretched into a week. The week became two.
So then the guy says to Geraldo, he goes, "It's a lifestyle choice, blah, blah..."
Can I sit on the couch for awhile?
uncomfortable chair

It's tough to adjust
to having someone in yor home.
Do you believe they changed actresses on "Roseanne?" Like no one's gonna notice!
Are you just going to leave those toe-nails on the floor?

Especially in yor bathroom.
Could you please explain how my toothbrush got in the toilet?
CHIPS

We went out a lot.
I introduced him to some girls from work.
I think they thought he was a little weird.
Peter's from Iowa City.
PLAY SOME AC/DC!!
PLAY AC/DC DAMN YOU!

We went on a camping trip to Big Sur.
Look how beautiful it is!
Pull over soon. We're out of jerky.
1

He got me addicted to Sega hockey. One night we stayed up 'til 5 a.m. trying to win the Stanley Cup.
Why won't he shoot? I'm pressing "B" and he won't shoot! This computer is defective I tell you!
You're supposed to press "C".

All the constant entertaining was killing me. My work started to suffer.
Another script about a houseguest that won't leave? Explain to me how this is gonna sell pizza!

I had to get him out of there.
Yaaaawn. Think I'll be hitting the sack.
You sure don't know how to party anymore.

But some people just can't take a hint.
Looks like winter's a-comin. Guess you'll be headed home soon.
Do you feel like a burrito?

It can be hard to tell a good friend he's over stayed his welcome.
What are you trying to say?
You! Go! Now!

He seemed to take it okay though.
See you in a month.
I'll be here.

After Peter left I was looking forward to some peace and quiet. But my neighbor plays her stereo too loud.
Goddam it!
BA-DA BOOMP BOOMP BOOMP

And it's always the Grateful Dead. I hate the Grateful Dead.
Hang on, Mom... SHAAAD-UP!
Friend of the devil is a friend of mine

Last night I put my boombox Face down on the floor and we had a stereo war. Nirvana vs. The Dead!
Let's just see how you like this! Heh-heh.

I'm not big on face to face confrontations though.
Could you turn your music down? I'm having a party.
Okay. Sorry.

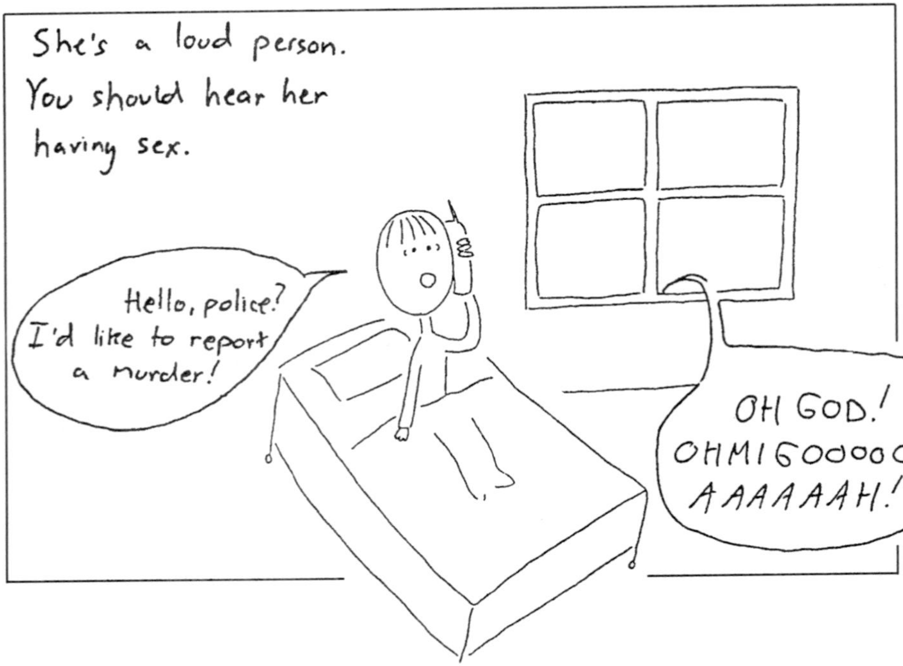

She's a loud person. You should hear her having sex.

Hello, police? I'd like to report a murder!

OH GOD! OHMIGOOOOOOD AAAAAAH!

I bought a pair of big construction boots. I'd goose-step down the hallway.
Eins! Zwei! Eins! Zwei!
clomp!
clomp!
Truckin' on a one-way street

It didn't do any good though. She's still as loud as ever.
Goddam it!
BA-DA BOOMP BOOMP BOOMP

There's this guy at work..
He's really starting to bug me too.
Woohoo! Just got 16,000 in Tetris
I got 18,000 yesterday.

The bosses love him. They're always joking around with him.
Ha, ha, ha! That's great, Chuck Ha, ha, ha!
I don't see what's so damn funny
SPORTS

The other day they sent this memo around about how he'd landed the company a huge new account.
MAIL
In Praise of Chuck
Damn.

I suppose he thinks that makes him cool or something.
Hey, guys! what's up?
I just got 22,000 in Tetris. That's what's up.

I came into work the other day. Chuck was moving his things.
Could you grab that certificate of achievement for me, man?

They gave him a window office. I couldn't believe it.
What's that blinding light?
That's called the "sun."

I went back and wrote a blistering resignation letter to the boss. It was all so unfair!
tap tap
tap
tap
tap

Of course I wimped out and never sent it.
DINER
... I mean the guy's nothing but a brown nose!
Does this tuna taste funky to you?

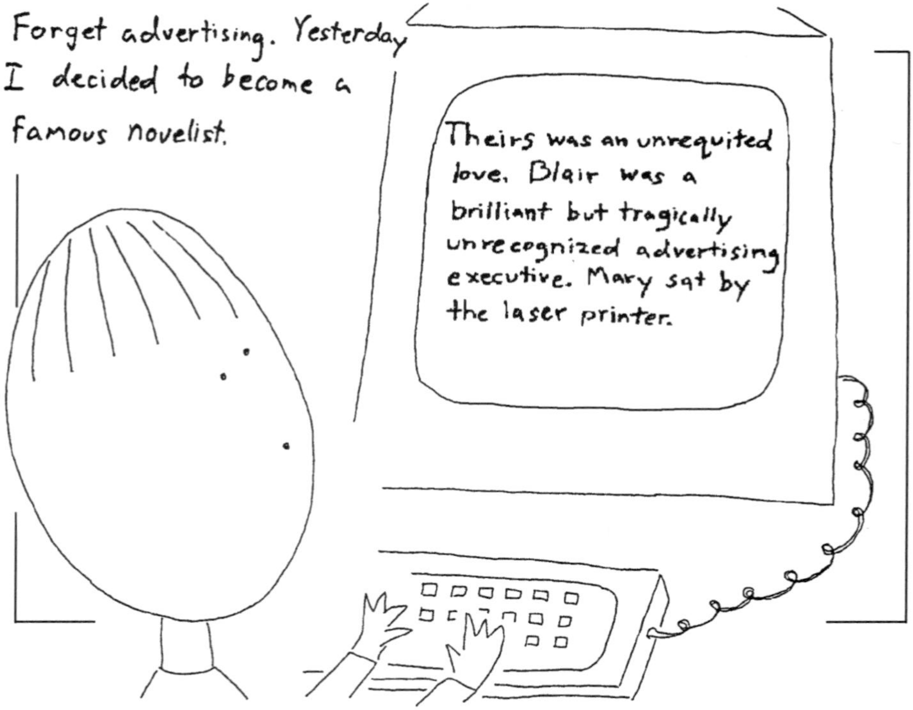

Forget advertising. Yesterday I decided to become a famous novelist.

Theirs was an unrequited love. Blair was a brilliant but tragically unrecognized advertising executive. Mary sat by the laser printer.

On weekends I'd wander the apartment in my bathrobe carrying a snifter of brandy.
The novelist at work.

I was inspired with a righteous indignation. Was this not the same divine muse of Tolstoy? Of Hemingway?
I'll show that stupid Chuck!

The other day I read a biography of F. Scott Fitzgerald. I'm trying to prepare for my new life.
Boy, could that guy party.

I decided I'm too boring. It was time for some action.
C'mon! Let's go dive into the stream of life!
Are you mad.? Baywatch is on.!

I resolved to act like my new heroes.
You made me spill my drink!
EXIT
What would Hemingway do in this situation?

Being a famous novelist is hard.
I think we can just catch the last ten minutes.

I'm having trouble writing.
I'm easily distracted.
Hello? No! No! I can talk.

I keep finding things around the house that need to be fixed.
click
Looks like that'll have to be totally rewired.

Suddenly I'm like, Joe Handyman.
ACE
ACE
...and why don't ya throw in a set of them socket wrenches?
ACE

Yesterday I made a set of really cool shelves.
Maybe I could be a famous carpenter

So I finally finished
my first chapter.
Rough. But undeniably
the work of a genius.

I passed it around to
some people at the office.
And I'm dedicating
it to you.

I guess I don't take
criticism very well.
Well, what the hell
do you know anyway?

I'll probably be one of those
geniuses that are recognized
after they're dead.
What's another phrase
for "tastes delicious?"
Yummy?

Last week I went home to Wisconsin for the 4th of July.
WAAAAAAH
zzzzz

My brother picked me up at the airport. He talked about engines the whole way home.
...and then I put in a 450 4-barrel with fuel-injection. She goes like nobody's business.

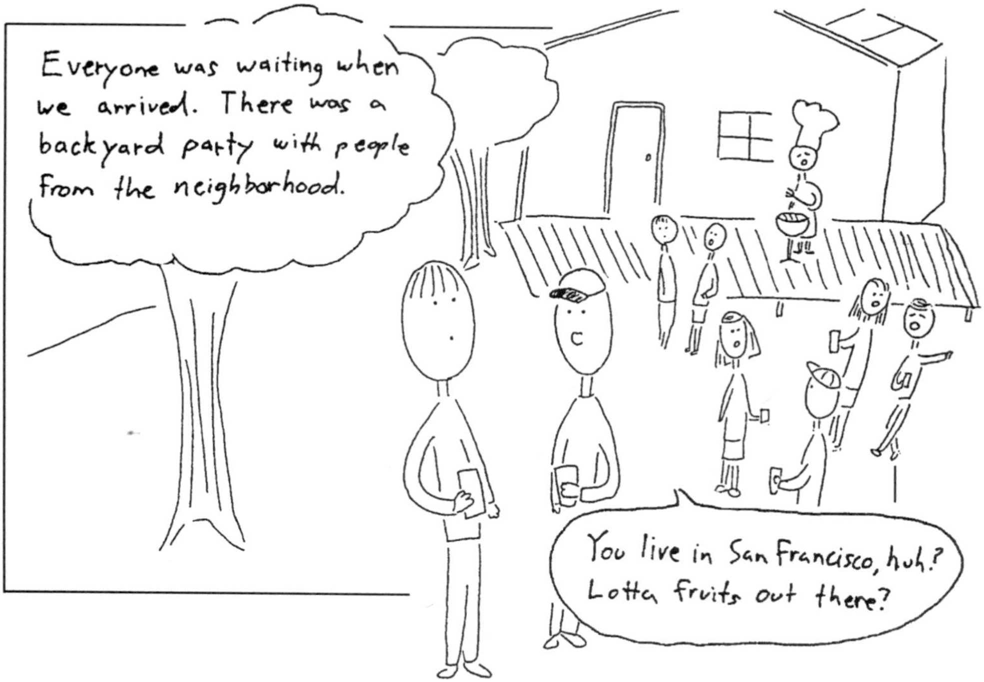

Everyone was waiting when we arrived. There was a backyard party with people from the neighborhood.

You live in San Francisco, huh? Lotta fruits out there?

I called my old girlfriend, Cathy. We always go out when I'm back in town.
So, have you found yourself in California yet?
No. But check out this new dance move.

We lived together once. But we used to get in fights and break things.
BAR
You still owe me for that official Green Bay Packer lamp!
Will you get over the stupid lamp?

We always talk about getting back together.
There's never been anyone for me but you.
Gimme your keys, Mr. Drunk and Sentimental.

But I don't know if we're ready yet.
This song sucks.
Touch that dial and I break your thumb.

I love being home.
My mom turns down my bed
and leaves me notes.
...And even though you're rapidly approaching thirty, balding slightly, and not yet married, we all still love you.

Sometimes, late at night, I'll go into the Kitchen and contemplate the Momosity of it all.
fully stocked fridge. No rancid milk
no dishes in sink
Wow.
no urine or vomit stains on floor
no chew cups or beer bottles

She's also great when I'm sick.
I try to take advantage of this.
Here's some jello and the new Sports Illustrated
me hungover

But sometimes she embarrasses me in front of my friends.
Good news, honey. I got the scooter marks out of your underwear.
heh-heh
Scooter marks?

I was trying to take a nap yesterday but my dad kept doing chores really loud.
crrrrrrrr

I mean, it was just one thing after the other.
Vvvvvvvv

I don't think he can stand the sight of me taking it easy.
BAM! BAM! BAM!

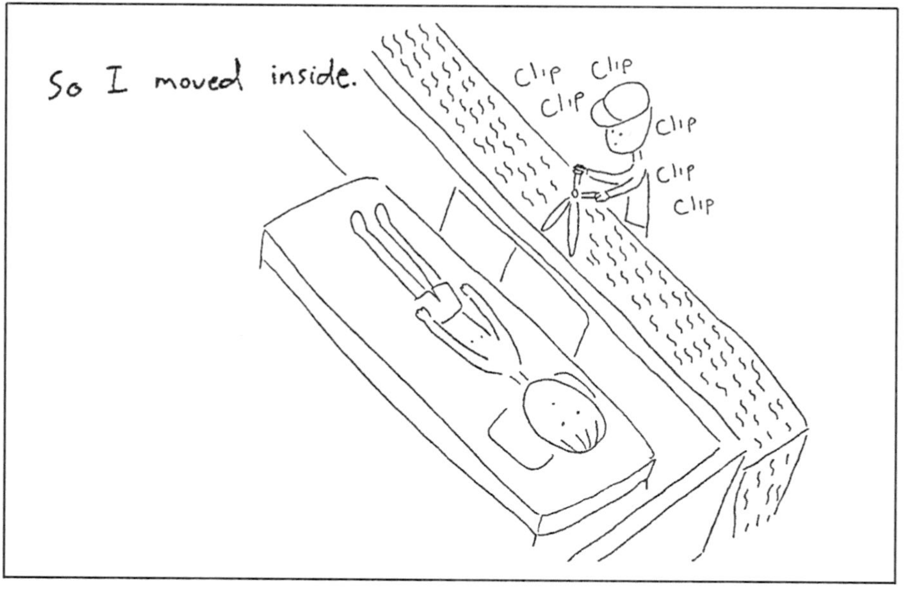
So I moved inside.
Clip Clip Clip Clip Clip Clip

The whole family went out for dinner one night. I drove.
Honey, look ooooout!
I see the car, mom.
My dad kept sending his steak back. He always embarrasses us in restaurants.
The squeaky wheel gets the grease.
Eat the damn steak, Henrik!

Then we went to see a movie.
I hate it when sex scenes come on and you're with yar parents.
I have to go to the bathroom.
Does he have a bladder problem now or what?

We capped it all off with a heated argument on the way home.
I see the car, mom.
And if Reagan were still in office, he'd sure as hell do something about it!

I think my dad's losing it a little. He's been muttering lately.
What's that, dad?
Fzzm! Krzzlp Flurz dozzzmplet!

Sometimes he'll walk into a room with a hammer or something, stop, look puzzled, and then walk out.

I suppose it's just part of the aging process.
Who the hell stole my reading glasses?

I just hope it doesn't happen to me.
SPEEDWAY BAR
Wha'd you say?
Fzzn! Flada bzzlmpn. Szzt!

On the 4th we had a big neighborhood softball game. My family is very competitive in these things.
Pssst. Brush 'er back.
Dad she's six years old.!

Then we grilled up huge steaks.
This isn't done quite right.
Eat it.

My brother drank a case of beer and broke out the fireworks.
W
Showtime!
FIREWORKS
I spent the rest of the 4th in the emergency room. It's the same thing every year.
St. Mary's ER
The doctor says he can save the finger but he'll have to operate.
Alright! You guys get HBO now?

When I got back to San Francisco my alumni newsletter was waiting. Seemed like everyone was married and settled.
Doug Allen is a doctor?! That guy puked on me once.
LU
TODAY

I called one of my old friends. He used to call himself "Mr. Party."
So, what's new with you, madman?
Um... I just finished painting my deck.

I started to get a little melancholy. I had to get a life.
I'll probably die alone.

Then Dave came over.
Dude! Let's start a rock band and get chicks!
Okay.

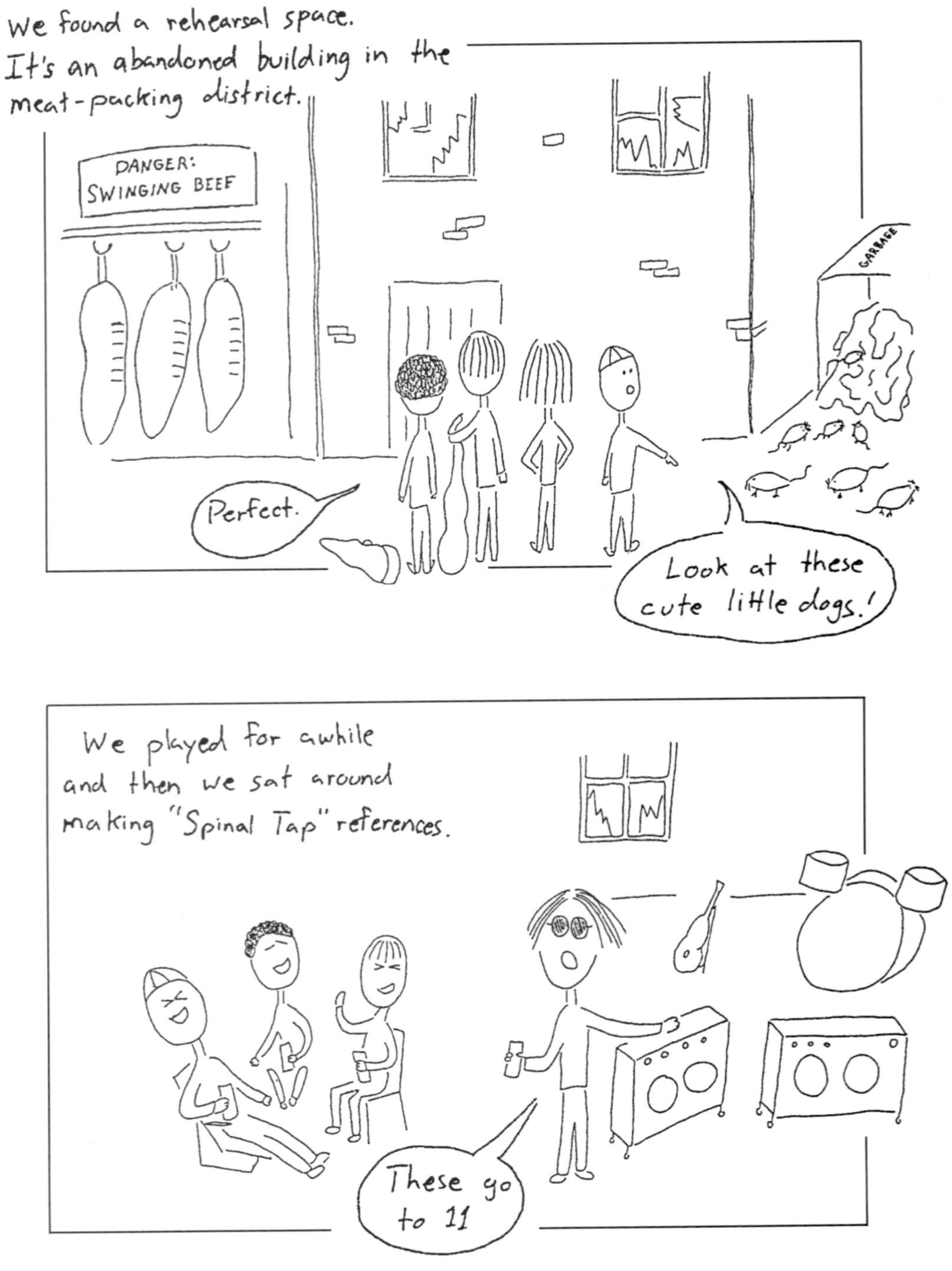

We found a rehearsal space.
It's an abandoned building in the meat-packing district.

DANGER:
SWINGING BEEF

Perfect.

GARBAGE

Look at these cute little dogs!

The only bad part is packing up the equipment at the end of the night.
And we could get mohawks and matching outfits!

It's also tough to work the next day.
Have you ever seen so much drool in your life?

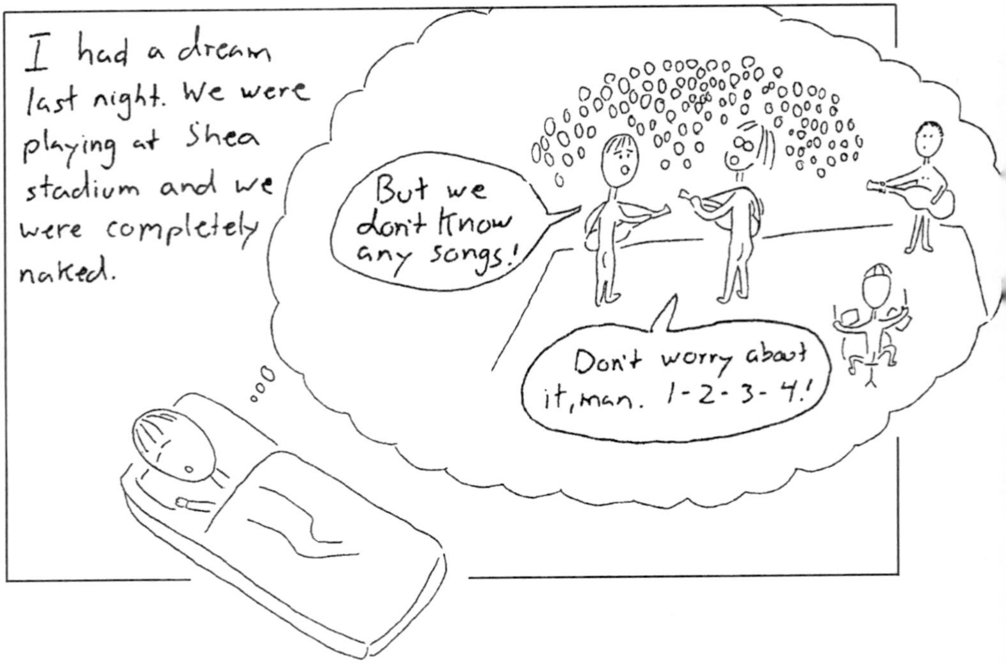

I had a dream last night. We were playing at Shea stadium and we were completely naked.

But we don't know any songs!

Don't worry about it, man. 1-2-3-4!

We practiced hard that week.
And then I'll say, "Does anyone here like to party?!!!"
And I'll say, "Yaaaah!"

Finally we were ready.
You're not gonna wear that shirt are ya?

The day of our show
I was really nervous.
puff
puff
Yeah, is this the Chronicle? I'm just a random rock fan calling to tell you about this great band playing tonight.

Everyone at work was excited for us.
slap
Rock 'n' roll!

But when we got to the club, the owner pulled a fast one on us.
CLU
And you guys will go on at 1:30.
A.M?!

All our friends went home.
Swinging BEEF
Does anyone here like to party?
Yaaaaah!

Got invited to another wedding.
I'm constantly going to weddings.
Tulsa in August sounds great!

I have to make a toast. I know, like, one joke and hate public speaking.
I could tell the one about the travelling salesman and the milking machine.

I bought a book: 1001 Great Wedding Toasts. None of them seemed quite right.
And as the thirteenth century monk Augustus the Pious once said...

I was sort of dreading the whole thing.
I heard about this guy who got so nervous he puked blood.

When I got to Tulsa it was about 110 degrees.
Sorry 'bout the air conditioning.
Phil's Cabs
Tulsa, Oklahoma

I was the first one to get to the hotel. I sat in the bar by myself.

Then I went up to my room to watch T.V. It only got two channels.
Soybeans are up 32 cents.

I was starting to wonder if I had the right weekend.
BAM
IOWA
ZZZZZZ
Tulsa! Are you ready to party?!!

Peter and I went down to the bar.
It was packed with people from school.
Good to see you again ...uh, dude!
It's Carl. We were roommates for two years.

It's amazing how much people change.
So, ultimately the heroin addiction led me to Jesus Christ Our Lord...
Mmm, hmm

My old girlfriend was there too.
With her husband.
And you're **still** single?
Yeah? So?!!

I got trapped in a lot
of bad conversations.
PD
PD
Technically, yes, I suppose you could call it a pyramid scheme. Do you think you might be interested?

We slept in the next morning.
I think the dry heaves are the part I like least.

Halfway through breakfast Peter had to go lie down in his car.
CAFE
Is he gonna want me to wrap that up to go?
I don't think so
CAT

I started to get nervous about my toast again.
Maybe I should go for a tearjerker.
Pull over right now!

We killed the afternoon at the hotel pool.
Two bloody marys. And look lively about it!
Perhaps a humorous poem.

The wedding was nice.
Shhhh!
Third bridesmaid from the right— I call!

But all through dinner I was freaking about my toast. How do I get into these things?
Are you allergic to cornish hen or something?

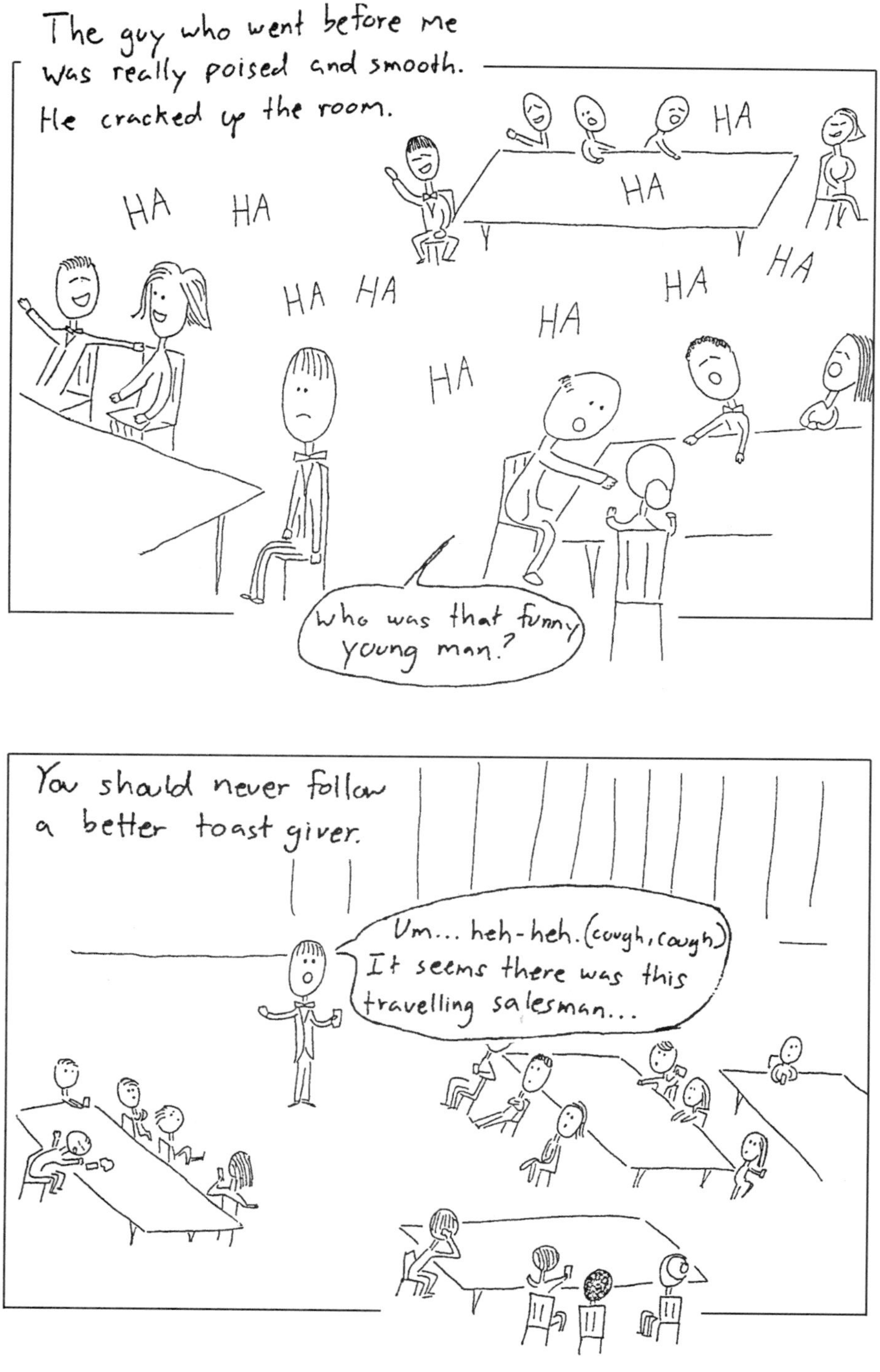

The guy who went before me was really poised and smooth. He cracked up the room.

HA HA HA HA HA HA HA HA HA HA HA

Who was that funny young man?

It was over. Finally I could relax and have fun.
It took some doing after that toast of yars but I've got some girls lined up.

That's when I met Elizabeth.
Peter tells me you're about to have a novel published? That's interesting.
What? Oh...uh, yeah.

I don't know if it was the tuxedo or the martinis but suddenly I thought I was Cary Grant.
Do you believe in destiny?

We went for a romantic walk on the golf course.
...and when I saw you this bitter, jaded ol' heart of mine said "23 Skidoo!"
You watch a lot of old movies, don't you?

Turns out she works for a magazine.
I tried to sound literary.
The moon has such a Proustian resonance this evening...
Uh... if you say so.

We held hands as I walked her to her room. Everything was going great.
Sorry about the sweaty palms.

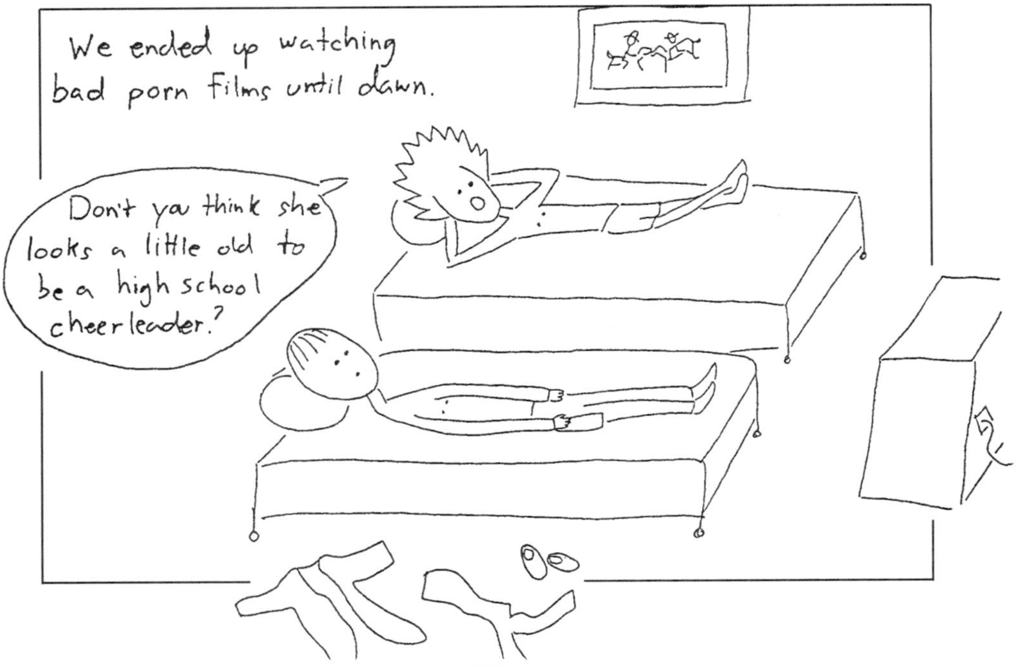

We ended up watching bad porn films until dawn.

Don't you think she looks a little old to be a high school cheerleader?

Forget women. It's fall again and time for manly pursuits like football.
He breaks into the secondary...

I got out all my football stuff.
Just a few inches taller and who knows?

Every Sunday a bunch of us get together for a big game. It's real macho stuff.
Those are fabulous! Do they come in white?

And the competition is fierce.
I call quarterback!
And whose ball will you be using?

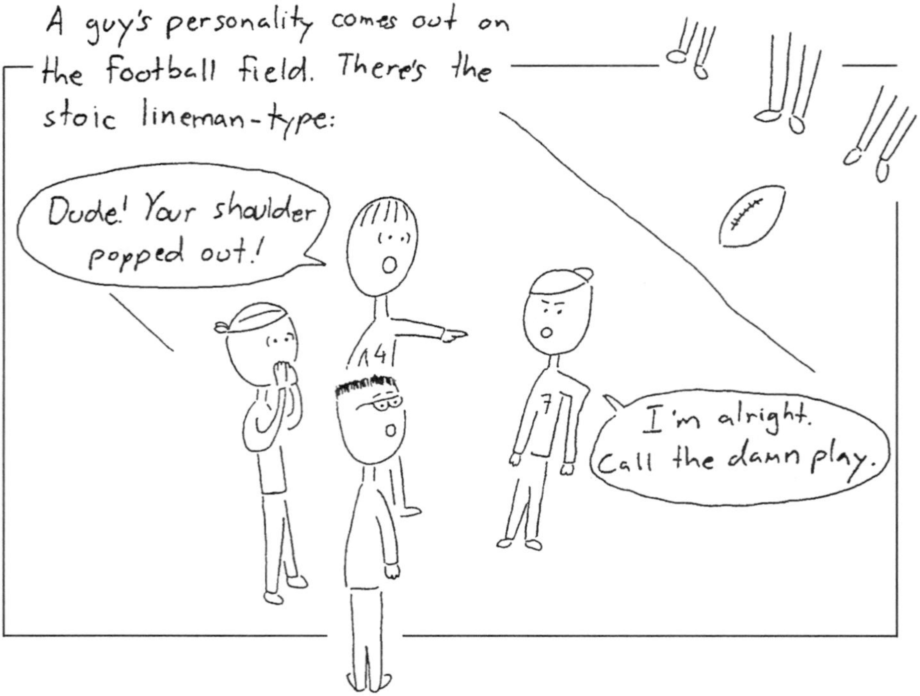

A guy's personality comes out on the football field. There's the stoic lineman-type:

Dude! Your shoulder popped out!

I'm alright. Call the damn play.

The cheating middle linebacker:
You're supposed to count to four Mississippi!
I was counting in my head.

And the egomaniacal quarterback:
And then I'll fade back and throw a spectacular pass to Larry. He then laterals back to me and I streak into the end zone. Okay? On two.

A lot of trash-talk goes on out there. White guys suddenly think they're black.
Don't chu be bringing that weak-ass shit in my house!
44
groan

Personal scores get settled.
Let's run this one at that girl-stealing Martin.
14
Again?
16

Since there's no refs
there's a lot of arguing.
Prove it.
Pass interference!

Usually resolved by what's known
as a "do-over."
I call "do-over."
Yeah. "Do-over."
That's the third
"do-over" this half!

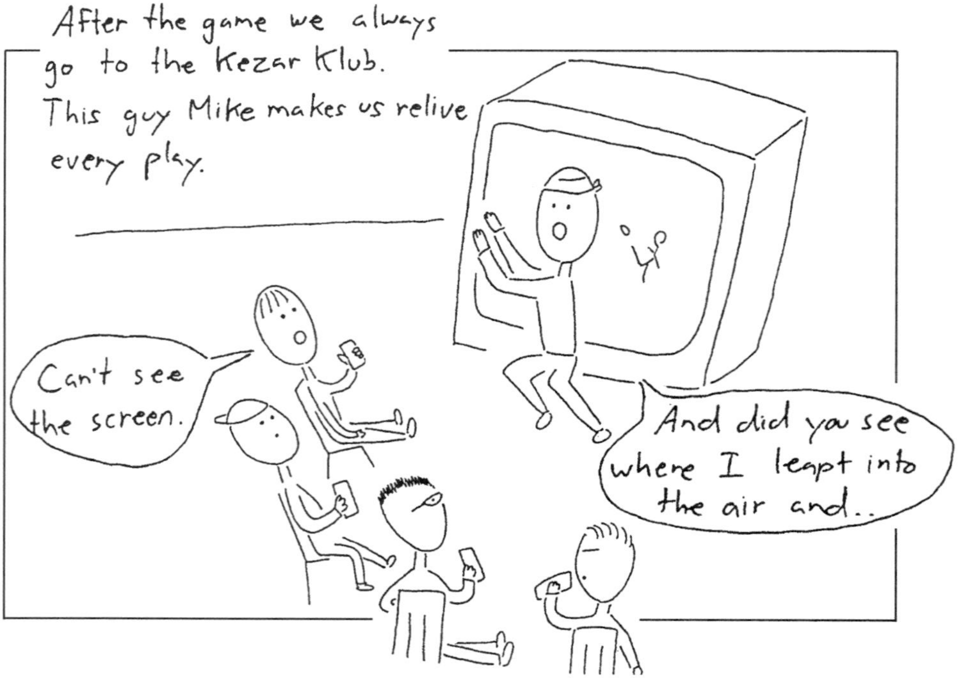

After the game we always go to the Kezar Klub. This guy Mike makes us relive every play.

Can't see the screen.

And did you see where I leapt into the air and...

Then we settle in and watch the pros.
Heaven on earth — a full day of football.
I'd have Reggie White's love-child if he asked me!

But you pay for it Monday morning.
Can't... move.

Man, was I sore from football.
I limped around the office all day
and took some muscle relaxants that night.

I had this weird dream.
My boss came into our office
and started raving in
some strange language.
Feelzaborp! Stp lin de Folubop!
Huh?

Then he changed into this
huge bird of prey. He kept
trying to peck out
my eyes.

I think I have a problem
with authority figures.
Hey, man! Howzit goin?
Aaaah!

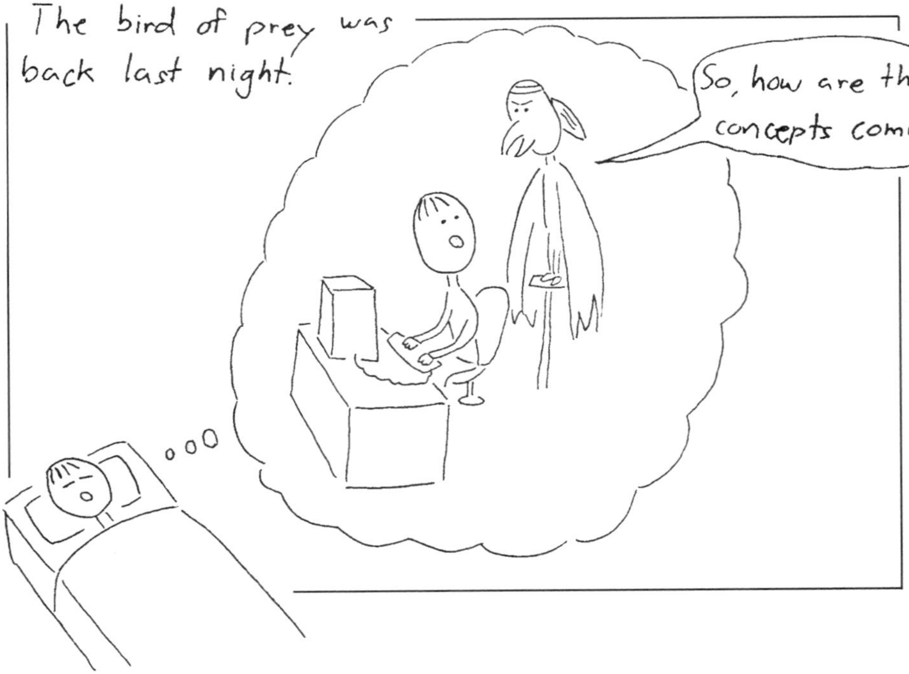

The bird of prey was back last night.

So, how are those concepts coming?

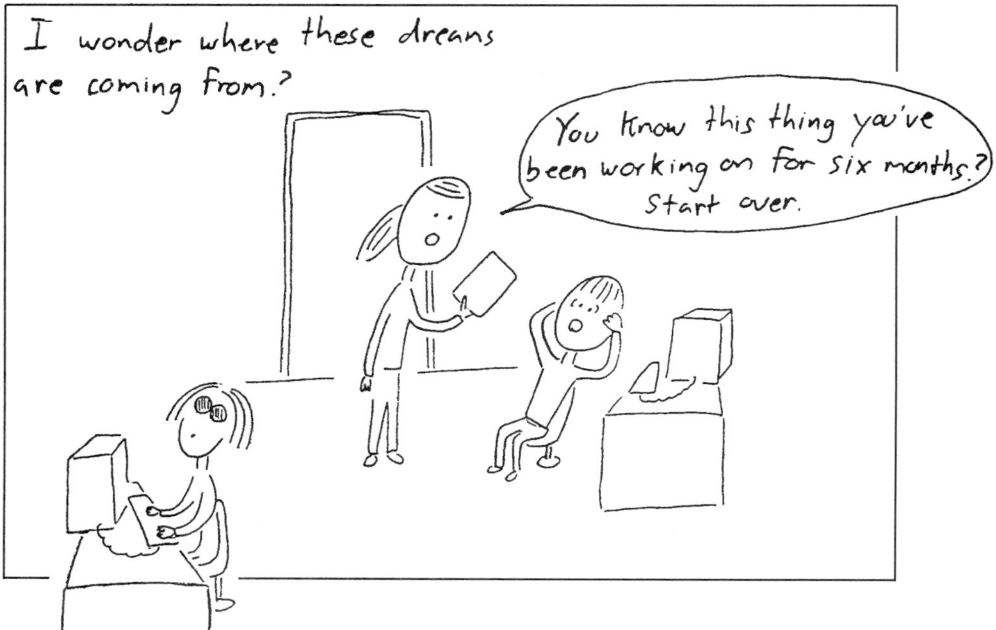

I wonder where these dreans are coming from?

You know this thing you've been working on for six months? Start over.

I've had it at work.
I get no respect at all.
BOSS
Can't he see? The idea is pure genius!
You misspelled the client's name again.

I decided to become a malcontent. I stopped shaving and wore bad-ass sunglasses.
Sort of look like Shaggy from Scooby-Doo.

I came when I pleased, I left when I pleased. And I just didn't care.
Uhhh... it's 10:30.
Really? I've got 10:45.

I guess it got a little out of hand.
Boss wants to see you.
What for?!!

I'm supposed to meet with the boss tomorrow.
And then I'll say, "It's high time, yes, high time I got some respect around here!"

All night the bird of prey circled my body.
ooo

But when he swooped down to peck out my eyes, he was repelled by my bad-ass sunglasses.
peck peck

I wasn't sure what to make of that one.
Maybe my subconscious defense mechanisms are wearing him down.
Maybe you don't like birds.

Stressville, U.S.A.
BOSS

He told me to knock it off with my new attitude. I thought I was going to be fired.
AWARD
AWARD
And frankly, you just look ridiculus!

But then, unbelievably, he gave me a small raise.
What the hell just happened?

I'd finally figured out how to get ahead in business.
And it all started with these sunglasses!
Let me see those babies.

Went to this movie the other night.
Four dollars for JuJu Bees? Hi-way robbery!

About half-way through it I got horrible stomach pains.
moan moan
It's not that bad
3

I sat in the bathroom for twenty minutes. It didn't help.
Definitely not Eddie Murphy's finest performance.
moooooaaan

I thought I was gonna die.
THEATER
COMING
JuJu Bee?

I made Dave drive me to the hospital.
I know it's around here somewhere.

The nurse could have been a little more sympathetic.
PACIFIC LUTHERAN
Fill this out
My Friend here has a stomach ache.
CAT

Finally they put me in a room and conducted a bunch of tests. The doctor kept calling me "Ace."
snap
Drop yar pants and bend over, Ace.

Let's just say I'm not a virgin anymore.
Noooo. Really? He did that?
Don't tell the guys on the softball team, okay? Okay?!!

It turns out I have kidney stones.
They're blocking my urinary tract.
And if you don't pass them your bladder might swell up and... KABLOOEY!
Just kidding, Ace.

They kept me overnight and gave me something for the pain.

I had to pass them.
But try as I might, I could not pee.

Who are you talking to in there?

C'mon big fella! You've never let me down before.

It was a rough one.
But I felt a lot better in the morning.
And I was thinking if you're not doing anything later...
Roll over please.

The doctor said I had to change my diet. No more milk and cheese!
Ace, you have the kidneys of a 78-year-old dairy farmer.

What a weird night that was.
PACIFIC LUTHERAN
Never did get to see the end of that movie.

I got a good story out of it though.
There I was... staring death straight in the eye!
Um... I have some work to do here...

Yesterday at work we got this important assignment.
AWARD
AWARD
AWARD
...and we'll be watching you guys closely on this one.
gulp
No problem, big guy!

We were nervous but excited. We got right to work.
What if we tried this idea where...
You hungry at all?

Our first efforts were not well received.
And then he eats the pizza and smiles. Whaddya think?
You guys are kidding about this, right?

So we went to the park and played whiffle ball.
Deeeep to right.!
Damn.

We were working hard, but nothing was coming.
Okay, let's say that if we don't make twenty catchrs in a row the world blows up. Go.

As the deadline approached, the creative juices really started to flow.
I could fake a seizure. Then they'd have to give it to someone else!
Hmmm. Not bad.

We finally came up with something late, late Sunday night.
Check it out, dude! I just made an origami bird!
Hey!

We lived to fight another day.
AWARD
AWARD
Well... I guess this doesn't completely suck.
Aaaay! We're your boys, big guy.

That weekend Dave came over.
We sat around watching old movies and drinking beer.
No offense but this is the most pathetic Friday night of my life.

Cary Grant was on.
Dahling!
Damn, that guy's suave!

He was committing jewel heists and seducing Grace Kelly. We were not.
What about that girl from the Liquor Barn? Did you ever call her?
Shot down in flames.

It was not a memorable evening.
What would Cary Grant do in this situation?
Martini?
shake shake

Yep, it was another lonely weekend. On Monday, Dave came up with a remarkable statistic.
February
According to my calculations, you have now gone 237 days without sex.
238.

He seemed to think this was some sort of superhuman feat.
Amazing, but true. There he is, ladies and gents!
Get outta here!

I was starting to get a complex about it. People were looking at me funny.
How are you? Really.
Why is everyone asking me that?

I mean, it's not like I'm not trying.
BAR
How'd it go?
The streak continues.

A streak is self-perpetuating. You exude what I call "the musk of desperation."
BAR
I'd like to talk to you but some instinctive force is telling me to go stand with my friends.

You feel dorky so you manifest it in all sorts of ways.
Whoa! Where'd you come up with that outfit?

I felt like a baseball player in a slump. I tried to analyze my swing—to nail the fundamentals.
Hello. It's very nice to meet you.

But when you're going bad you just don't get any bounces.
munch munch
You're eating a hot dog? You know an animal died in pain for that!!

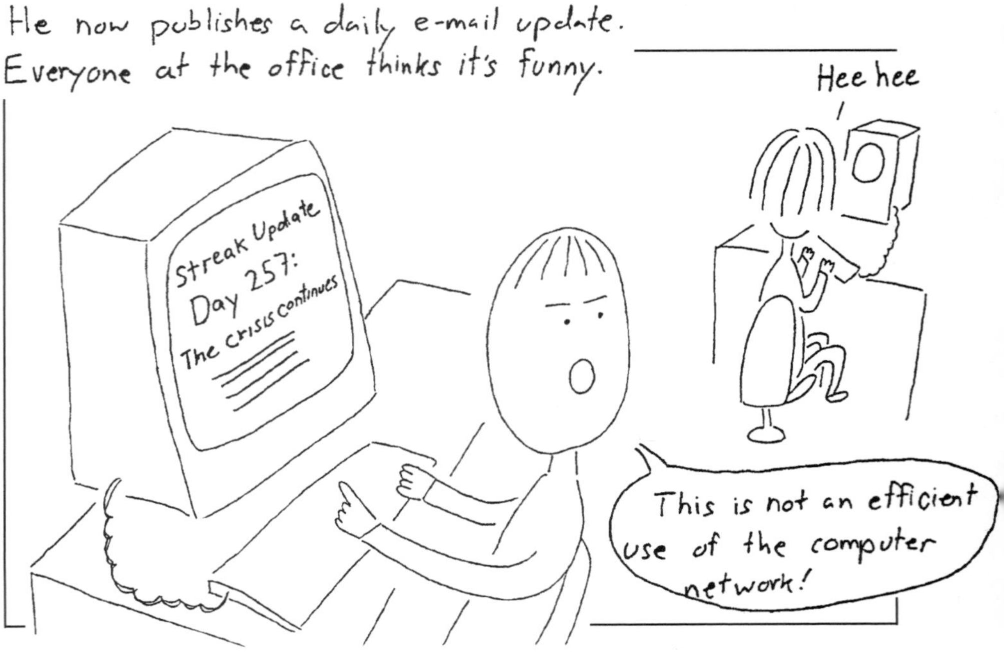

He now publishes a daily e-mail update. Everyone at the office thinks it's funny.

Hee hee

Streak Update Day 257: The crisis continues

This is not an efficient use of the computer network!

All the publicity was not helping my cause. One night I went to this party on the other side of town.

Wait a minute! You're the guy on that... that streak!

But after a while I sort of got caught up in the whole thing.

Streak-mania had reached a fever pitch. I brought in an outside consultant.
We'll have to start with your wardrobe.

He stressed the importance of cool hair. Women are powerless against cool hair.
Condition! Condition like the wind!

Martin worked with me for weeks.
Once more with feeling!
Hi! It's really nice to meet you!

Practice is one thing. But intangibles come into play in a game situation.
Hi, it's really nice to meet you.
Hi. Who's your cute friend?

I was desperate. I called my old girlfriend and offered to fly her in.
That's cheating!

Cathy arrived that Friday. I quickly explained the situation.
... and you can see the spot I'm in.
Mmm, hmm. What time's the next flight?

She got upset and said I was an insensitive pig. I had to kiss up for the rest of the weekend.
We just wanted a meal. We didn't want to buy the place!
BILL
Pay the man.

Joe Tour Guide.
And there's the stupid Golden Gate Bridge.
click

It wasn't a bad weekend though. And when I took her to the airport she suggested something.
B-6
Why don't you just make something up?

I took her advice.
Gather round!
I have an announcement.

I can tell a good story when I have to.

The streak was over.
My reputation was saved.
I heard about you! You're a sleazebag!
Thank you.

But after Cathy left, I kept finding myself thinking about her. Often, she'd be wearing a cheerleader outfit.
...and I want everyone's complete concentration on this...

I started calling her answering machine and leaving dorky messages.
Did that sound too anxious?
You might try to tone down the nervous laughter a bit.

I wrote her a long, passionate love letter to show her I was sincere.
sniff

And I even tried my hand at a few love poems. Once I left one in the office by mistake.
...The scent of lilies in the air, just like the shampoo you use on your hair.
Ha, ha. What's so funny, you guys?
HA
HA
HA
HA
HA

Finally, she started to come around.
MAIL
Hey, she wrote back.
Could be a restraining order.

Soon a long distance romance was in full swing.
I'll be in the vomitorium if anyone calls.
Aw, you wittow siwwy! Of course I miss my pootchikins.

Of course, because of our past, we had some important historical issues to clarify.
I did not flirt with Megan Shanahan at that party in '86! Dave, did I flirt with Megan Shanahan at that party in '86?
We had to turn the hose on you.

But eventually, we got it all worked out.
She's moving here. Do you believe it?
I give it three days, tops.

She arrived on a Tuesday.
I helped her unpack.
Wait a minute. You forgot your cheerleading outfit!
Pervert.

At first we were a little uncomfortable with the whole thing.
Hmmm. It just hit me. You have quit your job and moved across the country to be with me.
Yep. How soon will you be freaking out?

After all, we'd tried this before with somewhat disastrous results.
I'm warning you! Break that lamp and your clothes go out the window!
WISCONSIN, 1992

Still, this was a new era.
I think we've both grown since then, don't ya?
Oh, I know I've matured a great deal.

But I was happy to have her there. She's smart, she's pretty, she's only slightly unreasonable.
... and some new curtains there. Of course that couch will have to go.
Dream on, sister.

I did have to come to terms with the fact she was in town three days and got a better paying job than me.
That doesn't bother you, does it?
The fact the world values copier sales more than the work of a great artist? No. Why should it?

And really, it's been great to have someone to share all my time and interests with.
Magnum P.I. or the latest Robert Urich thing?
What an embarrassment of riches
TV

Yep, things are better these days. Except now it's a little more crowded on the couch.
Leg cramp!
You should exercise more.